3 Trace each word. Then match each word with its picture.

5 points each

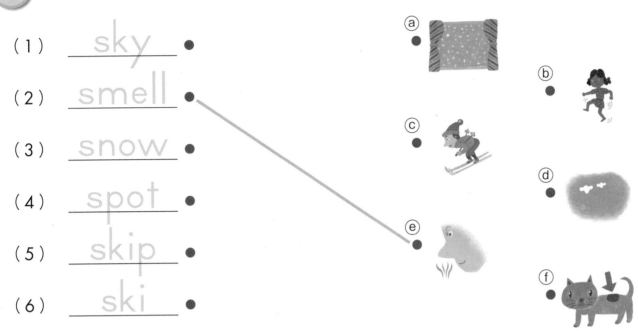

(1) _sky_ •

(2) _smell_ •

(3) _snow_ •

(4) _spot_ •

(5) _skip_ •

(6) _ski_ •

ⓐ
ⓑ
ⓒ
ⓓ
ⓔ
ⓕ

4 Complete each sentence with a word from the box.

4 points each

| sky | smell | snow | skip | ski |

(1) We jump in the _____.

(2) It is a star in the _____.

(3) We clap and _____.

(4) I _____ the fish.

(5) I _____ fast.

Good job!

Vocabulary
Consonant Combinations

3

Level ☆

Date / /

Name

Score /100

1 Trace the consonant combination to complete each word. Then read the word aloud. Match each word with its picture.

2 points each

(1)  sh ark •

(2) ch op •

(3) three •

(4) ch in •

(5) sh ip •

(6) th in •

(7) wh eel •

ⓐ •**3**...

ⓑ •

ⓒ •

ⓓ •

ⓔ •

ⓕ •

ⓖ •

2 Complete each word with a consonant combination from the box. You can use each combination more than once.

3 points each

| wh | sh | th | ch |

(1) ___ eel

(2)  ___ in

(3) ___ in

(4) ___ ark

(5) **3**... ___ ree

(6) ___ op

(7) ___ ip

3 Trace each word. Then read the word aloud.

(1)

hand

(2)

sick

(3)

lunch

(4)

whale

(5)

thick

(6)

fish

(7)

band

(8)

chair

4 Complete each sentence with a word from the box.

| band | lunch | sand | whale | chair |

(1) Put the _____ on a dish.

(2) I like to play in the _____.

(3) Please pick up the _____.

(4) We hear the _____.

(5) I see the _____.

You are good at this!

4

Level ☆

Date / /

Name

Score /100

1 Trace the letters to complete each word. Then match each word with its picture.

5 points each

(1) <u>c a n e</u> •

(2) <u>p l a n e</u> •

(3) <u>d a y</u> •

(4) <u>r a i n</u> •

(5) <u>b r a i n</u> •

(6) <u>b a y</u> •

ⓐ •

ⓑ •

ⓒ •

ⓓ •

ⓔ •

ⓕ •

2 Match each word from the box with its picture.

5 points each

bay	day	brain	plane	rain	cane

(1)

_____

(2)

_____

(3)

_____

(4)

_____

(5)

_____

(6)

_____

3 Trace each word. Then read the word aloud. Match each word with its picture.

4 points each

(1) bee •

(2) sea •

(3) feet •

(4) heat •

(5) three •

ⓐ •

ⓑ •

ⓒ •

ⓓ •

ⓔ • **3**•••

4 Complete each sentence with a word from the box.

4 points each

sea	feet	bee	three	heat

(1) There is a _____ near the tree.

(2) Ice cream melts in the _____.

(3) He sees _____ sheep.

(4) We swim in the _____.

(5) No _____ on the seat.

You did well!

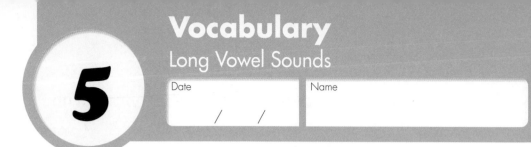

Vocabulary
Long Vowel Sounds

5

Level

Date   /   /

Name

Score   /100

1 Trace the letters to complete each word. Then read the word aloud.

3 points each

(1) hide

(2) cry

(3) kite

(4) slide

(5) hike

(6) five **5.....**

2 Match each word from the box with its picture.

4 points each

slide	hike	kite	cry	five	hide

(1) **5.....**

_____

(2)

_____

(3)

_____

(4)

_____

(5)

_____

(6)

_____

3 Trace each word. Then read the word aloud. Match each word with its picture.

4 points each

(1) bone •

(2) rope •

(3) boat •

(4) rose •

(5) goat •

(6) road •

(7) hole •

ⓐ •

ⓑ •

ⓒ •

ⓓ •

ⓔ •

ⓕ •

ⓖ •

4 Complete each sentence with a word from the box.

5 points each

bone	rope	boat	rose	goat	road

(1) A _____ eats grass.

(2) The _____ can float.

(3) She hoses the _____.

(4) His _____ is in the hole.

(5) We skip _____.

(6) We cross the _____.

Keep going!

11

6

1 Trace the vowels to complete each word. Then read the word aloud. Match each word with its picture.

4 points each

(1) blue •

(2) tune •

(3) glue •

(4) flute •

(5) cute •

(6) cube •

(7) dune •

ⓐ •

ⓑ •

ⓒ •

ⓓ •

ⓔ •

ⓕ •

ⓖ •

2 Complete each phrase with a word from the box.

4 points each

| dune | glue | cube |

(1) _____ in the tube

(2) a tune on the _____

(3) blue _____

3 Write the rhyming word to complete each rhyming pair.   5 points each

(1) blue _____

(2) play _____

(3) float _____

(4) see _____

(5) hike _____

(6) train _____

(7) dive _____

(8) toad _____

4 Complete each sentence with a word from the box.   5 points each

| wheel | train | nose | sky |

(1) Put the rose near your _____ .

(2) Birds fly in the _____ .

(3) It rains on the _____ .

(4) I feel the _____ .

You can write well!

7

Sight Words

Date
/   /

Name

Level
☆

Score
/100

1 Trace the word to complete each sentence.

5 points each

(1) ___The___ plane lands.

(2) ___The___ dog runs.

(3) ___This___ costs five dollars.

(4) ___This___ sock is dirty!

2 Trace the word on each rock in the stream. Then cross the stream by connecting the rocks that say "The."

20 points for completion

3 Trace the word to complete each sentence.

5 points each

(1) _____A_____ cat jumps.

(2) _____A_____ boy opens a book.

(3) _____An_____ ant climbs.

(4) _____An_____ ox is big.

(5) _____All_____ cats can climb.

(6) _____All_____ boys want to run.

4 Trace all the words. Then draw a line to connect the three boxes in a row that have the same word.

10 points for completion

all	an	a
all	all	an
an	a	all

5 Find each word from the box in one of the word jumbles below. Then write the word in the space provided.

5 points each

an	all	the	this

(1) a b x l y a l l x b _____

(2) p x t r h m t h i s _____

(3) b y o o k l a n p b _____

(4) u i w t h e l m n r _____

You can do it all!

8 Sight Words

Level

Score

Date / /

Name

/100

1 Trace the sight words to complete each sentence pair. Then read the sentences aloud.

5 points each

(1) Is that __a__ dog?   __Yes__, it is.

(2) Did you get __a__ cat?   __No__.

(3) Are they __all__ boys?   No, __not__ all.

(4) Is that __a__ plane?   __Yes__, it is.

2 Answer the following questions with "Yes" or "No."

6 points each

(1) Is that a dog?    _____.

(2) Did you get a cat?    _____.

(3) Are they all boys?    _____.

(4) Is that a plane?    _____.

3 Read each sentence aloud. Then circle each bold word in the sentence.

4 points each

(1) **the**   I sat on (the) chair.

(2) **an**   Do you want an apple?

(3) **this**   Is this my hat?

(4) **all**   No, not all birds can fly.

(5) **yes**   Yes, she likes to read.

(6) **no**   There is no soap.

4 Complete each sentence with a word from the box.

8 points each

an	all	this	a

(1) Is ____ your shoe?

(2) I swam in ____ ocean.

(3) He read ____ of the books.

(4) She plays ____ flute.

You are good!

Punctuation

1   Trace the word and period to complete each sentence.   *5 points each*

(1) The cake is sweet.

(2) The bat flew away.

(3) Cats lick their paws.

(4) Saturday is my birthday.

(5) The big dog ran.

(6) Amy is happy.

Don't forget!

A **sentence** begins with a *capital letter* and ends with a *period*.

---

2   Rewrite the letters below as a sentence with correct spacing, punctuation, and capital letters.   *4 points each*

(1) alldogsbark _____

(2) iliketoeatfish _____

(3) soccerisfun _____

(4) thesunisyellow _____

(5) thetentwaswet _____

3 Circle the sentences with correct punctuation and capital letters.

10 points for completion

My shirt is black.

the bat scared me

you have a dog

My doll is broken.

That's my favorite

I like candy.

Bob is funny.

lemons are not. sweet

4 Write capital letters and periods to complete the passage.

40 points for completion

__T__ he sun is out today__.__ __I__ t is hot __.__
(t)   (i)

___ e want to play tag with Timmy __
(w)

___ hat would be fun__
(t)

___ he game is starting__
(t)

___ immy fell down__
(t)

___ hope he is okay__
(i)

___ e is fine__
(h)

___ e can play again__
(w)

Keep it up!

© Kumon Publishing Co., Ltd.   19

Punctuation

Level ★★   Score /100

1 Trace each sentence. Then read it aloud.

6 points each

(1) The dog barks.

(2) Is this your pen?

(3) Is that my hat?

(4) That bee stung me!

(5) I hit my leg!

Don't forget!

A **period (.)** shows the end of a statement.
A **question mark (?)** shows the end of a question.
An **exclamation mark (!)** shows the end of an exclamation.

---

2 Complete the sentences with punctuation marks from each box.

5 points each

(1) Is that your pen___ Yes it is___ | ? | . |

(2) That bee stung me___ Are you okay___ | ? | ! |

(3) Is her shirt black ___ Her shirt is green ___ | . | ? |

(4) Where did you go this summer ___ | ? | . |
We went to the beach___

3 Complete each sentence with a punctuation mark from the box. You can use each punctuation mark more than once.

4 points each

! . ?

(1) The sea has saltwater in it ___

(2) Wow, that hurt ___

(3) What did you eat for dinner ___

(4) Happy birthday ___

(5) We ran home ___

4 Rewrite the letters below as a sentence with correct spacing, punctuation, and capital letters.

6 points each

(1) thatdogbitme

_____

(2) thetoybroke

_____

(3) donottouchthefire

_____

(4) isittimeforbed

_____

(5) ilikecarrots

Nice work!

_____

11

1 Write the name of each object below its picture.

3 points each

(1)
_____

(2)
_____

(3)
_____

(4)
_____

(5)
_____

(6)
_____

(7)
_____

(8)
_____

(9)
_____

(10)
_____

Don't forget!

Words that name people, places, or things are called **nouns**.
Nouns are "naming" words.

2 Match each noun with its sentence. Write the noun to complete each sentence.

6 points each

(1) cow •

•ⓐ The _____ hunts.

(2) tiger •

•ⓑ The _____ plays.

(3) girl •

•ⓒ The _____ moos.

3 Complete each sentence with a noun.

2 points each

(1) The <u>panda</u> eats.

(2) The _____ runs.

(3) The _____ stops.

(4) The _____ roars.

(5) The _____ is green.

(6) The _____ left.

4 Complete each sentence with a capital letter, noun, and period.

8 points each

(1) <u>T</u>he <u>lion</u> sleeps<u>.</u>

(2) ___he _____ walks__

(3) ___he _____ plays__

(4) ___he _____ climbs__

(5) ___he _____ is red__

Perfect!

Nouns
Plural

12

Level ★★

Date / /

Name

Score
/100

1 Trace each noun.

2 points each

(1)  dogs

(2) girls

(3) pigs

(4) pens

(5) cars

(6) balls

(7)  ants

(8) cows

Don't forget!

When there is more than one of something, the noun is **plural**.
Most plural nouns have an "s" on the end.

2 Which words describe more than one of something? Circle each plural noun.

20 points for completion

 crabs

 rabbits

 lamps

 roof

 zoo

 spoons

 boat

 coins

 bat

 tent

 plane

 pond

3 Is there more than one of each thing in each picture? If the noun should be plural, add an "s" on the end.

2 points each

(1) pigs

(2) cow

(3) panda

(4) bike

(5) girl

(6) boy

(7) swan

(8) car

(9) lion

(10) frog

(11) teacher

(12) pen

4 Complete each sentence with a singular or plural noun.

8 points each

(1) The _____ eat.

(2) The _____ sleeps.

(3) The _____ play.

(4) The _____ fall.

(5) The _____ drive.

Way to go!

Pronouns

Date   /   /

Name

Level
★ ★

Score
/100

---

1 Trace the pronoun to complete each sentence.

6 points each

(1) __I__ like books. Do you like books?

(2) The boy is sad. __He__ has no books.

(3) The girl is happy. __She__ has a book!

(4) Those kids read. __They__ like libraries.

(5) The book is big. __It__ is black.

Don't forget!

A **pronoun** is a word that stands for a noun.
    For example: *Jon* likes gum. / *He* likes gum.

---

2 Match each picture with its pronoun.

30 points for completion

(1) •   • ⓐ he

(2) •   • ⓑ she

(3) •   • ⓒ they

(4) •   • ⓓ it

3 Replace the bold words with a pronoun from the box. 5 points each

She	It	He	They

(1) **The girl** swims fast. _____ swims fast.

(2) **The kids** race. _____ race.

(3) **My dad** is tall. _____ is tall.

(4) **The pool** is big. _____ is big.

4 Complete each sentence with a pronoun from the box. 5 points each

He	She	It	They

(1) The book is large. _____ is heavy.

(2) Lisa runs home. _____ is fast!

(3) Jon drinks water. _____ is thirsty.

(4) The boys play tag. _____ run away.

You are doing well!

27

1 Trace each pronoun to complete each sentence.

30 points for completion

(1) I have a book. The book is my book.

(2) She has a ball. The ball is her ball.

(3) He has a bat. The bat is his bat.

(4) You have a cat. The cat is your cat.

2 Replace the bold words in each sentence with a pronoun from the box.

5 points each

my	his	your	her

(1) **The boy** has a box.
The box is his box.

(2) I have a flute.
The flute is _____ flute.

(3) **She** has a big dog.
The big dog is _____ dog.

(4) **You** have red paint.
The red paint is _____ paint.

3 Trace each pronoun to complete each sentence.

30 points for completion

(1) I have a bat. The bat is mine.

(2) She has a mouse. The mouse is hers.

(3) He has a hat. The hat is his.

(4) You have a chair. The chair is yours.

4 Replace the bold word in each sentence with a pronoun from the box.

5 points each

mine	his	yours	hers

(1) **You** have a kite.
The kite is yours.

(2) **She** has a blue coat.
The blue coat is _____.

(3) **He** has a red hat.
The red hat is _____.

(4) **I** have a green shirt.
The green shirt is _____.

You got it!

Pronouns

1 Match the sentences according to the pronouns.

30 points for completion

(1) **I** am locked out. •

•ⓐ Please hug **him**.

(2) **He** is sad. •

•ⓑ Please help **her**.

(3) **She** is lost. •

•ⓒ Please let **me** in.

(4) **Your** bag is open.•

•ⓓ Can **you** close it?

2 Complete each sentence with a word from the box.

5 points each

you	him	her	me

(1) I am hungry.
Come with _____ to lunch!

(2) Your glass is empty.
Do _____ want more?

(3) Mary is going home.
Say good-bye to _____.

(4) John went outside.
The cat followed _____.

3 Trace the pronoun to complete each sentence. 5 points each

(1) Sam and I run. <u>We</u> run fast!

(2) Tali and Jane play ball. <u>They</u> are good!

(3) Dad and I are hungry. <u>We</u> make lunch.

(4) My cats are lazy. <u>They</u> like to nap.

4 Complete each sentence with a word from the box. 5 points each

me	you	We	they	him	her

(1) I see Bo and Lane over there.
Will ____ play with me?

(2) Sally talks very loudly.
I can hear ____ in the next room.

(3) My sister and I jog a mile.
____ like to run.

(4) This is not my coat.
Does it belong to ____?

(5) Matt just left.
Catch up with ____.

(6) This is my lunch.
It is for ____.

Good job!

31

16

Verbs
Singular

Date / /

Name

Level ★★

Score /100

1 Trace the verb to complete each sentence.   5 points each

(1) The tiger drinks.   (2) The dog eats.

(3) The cat runs.   (4) The frog jumps.

(5) The horn blows.   (6) A boy rows.

> **Don't forget!**
> Words used to describe actions are called **verbs**. Verbs are "doing" words.

2 Complete each sentence with a verb from the brackets.   5 points each

(1) The plant _____.   [grows / sings]

(2) Mom ____ the food.   [roars / chops]

(3) That button ____.   [pops / sleeps]

(4) The cowboy ____.   [rides / rows]

3 Match each sentence with its picture.

4 points each

(1) The panda eats. •

(2) The boy walks. •

(3) The tiger sleeps. •

(4) The bell rings. •

(5) The boy falls. •

ⓐ

ⓑ

ⓒ

ⓓ

ⓔ

4 Complete each sentence with a verb.

6 points each

(1) The dog _____.

(2) The boy _____.

(3) The lion _____.

(4) The pig _____.

(5) My brother _____.

Hooray!

Verbs
Plural

Date / /

Name

Score

/100

1 Trace each plural verb. Then read the sentence pair aloud.   5 points each

(1) The mother smiles. / The mothers smile.

(2) The skunk smells. / The skunks smell.

(3) The whale jumps. / The whales jump.

(4) The pencil breaks. / The pencils break.

(5) The lion roars. / The lions roar.

(6) The girl sings. / The girls sing.

(7) The cowboy rides. / The cowboys ride.

Don't forget!

When the noun is plural, the verb also must be **plural**. Most plural verbs do <u>not</u> have an "s" on the end.

    For example: The cat *sleeps*. / The cats *sleep*.

---

2 Circle each sentence with a plural noun and verb.   15 points for completion

The drink spills.   The hot dogs fall.

The frogs jump.   The trumpet blows.

The stars shine.   The ballerinas turn.

3 Match the sentence parts.   5 points each

(1) The zebras •   •ⓐ jumps into the pond.

(2) The frog •   •ⓑ play.

(3) The bell •   •ⓒ run in the field.

(4) The girls •   •ⓓ rings.

4 Complete each sentence with a verb from the brackets.   5 points each

(1) The baby sleeps.   [sleep / sleeps]

(2) The girls _____ tag.   [play / plays]

(3) The kittens _____ soft. [feels / feel]

(4) My brother _____ books. [read / reads]

(5) The airplanes _____.   [land / lands]

(6) The racer _____ fast.   [drives / drive]

Good job!

18

Date / /

Name

Level ★★

Score

/100

---

1 Match the sentence parts.

5 points each

(1) The car •

(2) The boats •

(3) The watch •

(4) The girls •

•ⓐ is broken.

•ⓑ turns.

•ⓒ play.

•ⓓ float.

---

2 Complete each sentence with a verb from the brackets.

6 points each

(1) The stars _____ in the sky. [shine / shines]

(2) The boy _____ in his bed. [sleep / sleeps]

(3) The goat _____ grass.   [eat / eats]

(4) Three birds _____ in the tree. [land / lands]

(5) The snake _____ for food. [hunt / hunts]

3 Complete each sentence with a verb from the box. Make it singular if necessary.

5 points each

play   fall   run   float

(1) The leaf _____ from the tree.

(2) My brother _____ for the ball.

(3) The boys _____ with their trucks.

(4) Her toy boat _____.

4 Write an "s" after each noun that should be plural.

5 points each

(1) The <u>bee</u> fly to the rose.

(2) A <u>cone</u> is in the road.

(3) My dog has two <u>spot</u>.

(4) We see three <u>hog</u> run.

(5) My <u>bag</u> is lost.

(6) The <u>ant</u> march to the food.

Way to go!

19

1 Trace the verb to complete each sentence.   4 points each

(1) I _run_ .

(2) I _jump_ .

(3) I _sleep_ .

(4) I _hit_ the ball.

(5) I _fall_ down.

> ## Don't forget!
> Verbs in a sentence with the pronoun "I" are called **first-person singular** verbs. Most first-person singular verbs do <u>not</u> have an "s" at the end.

2 Complete each sentence with a verb from the brackets.   6 points each

(1) I _cook_ .   [cooks / cook]

(2) I _____ .   [fall / falls]

(3) I _____ dinner.   [eats / eat]

(4) I _____ my shirt.   [finds / find]

(5) I _____ a book.   [read / reads]

3 Trace the verb to complete each sentence.

4 points each

(1) The jar falls. (2) He runs.

(3) She jumps. (4) The car stops.

(5) My hand hurts.

> **Don't forget!**
>
> A verb in a sentence with the pronoun "he," she," or "it" is a **third-person singular** verb. Most third-person singular verbs have an "s" at the end.

4 Complete each sentence with the verb in the brackets. Add an "s" at the end of each verb.

5 points each

(1) She _____. [yell]

(2) The lady _____. [sleep]

(3) The man _____. [cook]

(4) He _____. [eat]

(5) It _____. [break]

(6) The robot _____. [move]

You are great!

20

Verbs
First, Second, and Third Person

Date   /   /

Name

Level
★★

Score
/100

1 Trace the verb to complete each sentence.   2 points each

(1) You run .

(2) You stop .

(3) You sleep .

(4) You like apples.

(5) You ride your bike.

> **Don't forget!**
> A verb in a sentence with the pronoun "you" is a **second-person singular** verb. Most second-person singular verbs do <u>not</u> have an "s" at the end.

2 Complete each sentence with a verb from the brackets.   5 points each

(1) You cook .   [cooks / cook]

(2) You _____ glue.   [use / uses]

(3) You _____ water.   [drinks / drink]

(4) You _____ by the slide.   [hide / hides]

(5) You _____ lunch.   [eats / eat]

(6) You _____ your book.   [read / reads]

3 Complete each sentence with a verb from the brackets. 5 points each

(1) I _____ .   [sleep / sleeps]

(2) I _____ fast.   [run / runs]

(3) You _____ on the chair.   [sit / sits]

(4) You _____ on the step.   [trip / trips]

(5) He _____ far.   [jump / jumps]

(6) She _____ water.   [drink / drinks]

4 Complete each sentence with a verb from the box. 6 points each

drops	like	play	swims	looks

(1) I _____ cards.

(2) She _____ at the tree.

(3) He _____ the ball.

(4) Do you _____ apples?

(5) Maggie _____ fast!

Wow! Well done.

21

Verbs
Am / Are / Is

Level ★★

Date / /

Name

Score /100

1 Trace the verb to complete each sentence.   5 points each

(1) I _am_ tired.   (2) You _are_ happy.

(3) He _is_ home.   (4) She _is_ on the slide.

> **Don't forget!**
> The verb "to be" is not like other verbs. It is an irregular verb. "To be" can become "am," are," or "is." Pay special attention to the way it changes!

2 Complete each sentence with a verb from the brackets.   5 points each

(1) I _am_ tall.   [am / is / are]

(2) I ____ happy.   [am / is / are]

(3) You ____ my dad.   [am / is / are]

(4) You ____ silly.   [am / is / are]

(5) He ____ in the pool.   [am / is / are]

(6) She ____ funny.   [am / is / are]

3 Match the sentence parts.

(1) She •   •ⓐ are on a bike.

(2)  You •   •ⓑ is happy.

(3)  I •   •ⓒ is on a chair.

(4) He •   •ⓓ am sad.

4 Complete each sentence with a verb from the box.

is	are	am	is	am

(1) I <u>am</u> tall.

(2) Dave ____ short.

(3) You ____ fast!

(4) I ____ hot.

(5) The dog ____ small.

Keep it up!

43

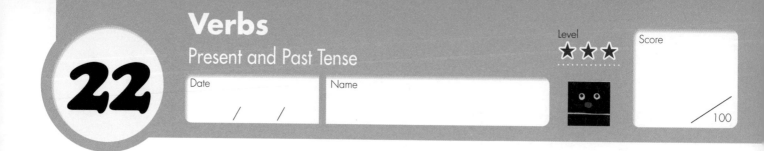

Verbs
Present and Past Tense

22

Date / /

Name

Level ★★★

Score

/100

1 Trace the verb to complete each sentence. Then read the sentence aloud.

5 points each

(1) The truck stops.   (2) My cat sleeps.

(3) My team wins.   (4) Dad shaves.

2 Trace the verb to complete each sentence. Then read the sentence pair aloud.

6 points each

(1) Jane waves. / Jane waved yesterday.

(2) Father cooks. / Father cooked last night.

(3) I want candy. / I wanted candy yesterday.

(4) The deer jumps. / The deer jumped earlier.

(5) We play. / We played yesterday.

Don't forget!

We use different forms of verbs to show *when* something happens. If it is happening *now*, the verb is in the **present** tense. If something has happened *before*, the verb is in the **past** tense. Usually, verbs in the past tense end in "ed."

    For example: The cat *jumps*. / Yesterday the cat *jumped*.

3 Add "ed" to change each verb to the past tense.   5 points each

(1) I wanted ice cream.

(2) He paint___ the wall.

(3) The children talk___.

(4) She walk___ home.

(5) My brother add___ the numbers.

(6) We wait___ for the bus.

4 Complete each sentence with a verb from the brackets.   5 points each

(1) Do you _____ to play with me?
   [want / wants / wanted]

(2) My brother _____ his food last night.
   [share / shares / shared]

(3) The girl _____ earlier.
   [play / played]

(4) The boy _____ yesterday.
   [walk / walks / walked]

Great job!

45

1 Complete each sentence with the verb in the past tense.   5 points each

(1) The boys collect shells.
The boys _____ shells.

(2) The men sail on the sea.
The men _____ on the sea.

(3) The women work.
The women _____ .

2 Complete each sentence with a verb from the brackets.   10 points each

(1) We _____ in the park yesterday.
[walk / walks / walked]

(2) My uncle _____ breakfast last week.
[cook / cooks / cooked]

(3) Sam _____ over a log earlier.
[jump / jumps / jumped]

(4) I _____ my teeth last night.
[brush / brushed]

3 Match the sentence parts.

5 points each

(1) Last week, I •

•ⓐ kicked the ball hard.

(2) Earlier Spot •

•ⓑ play tag!

(3) Yesterday, he •

•ⓒ licked me.

(4) We •

•ⓓ spilled juice.

4 Complete each sentence with a verb from the box.

5 points each

| tripped | call | pulled | poke | helped |

(1) She _____ her mom earlier.

(2) Can you _____ the doctor?

(3) This morning we _____ weeds.

(4) Yesterday, Jon _____ .

(5) Do not _____ me!

You finished that fast!

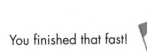

47

Review
Verbs

Level
★ ★ ★

Date
/   /

Name

Score
/100

1 Rewrite each sentence in the past tense.   5 points each

(1) The girls paint.

The girls painted.

(2) Mom dusts the chair.

_____

(3) The show ends.

_____

(4) Billy adds one and one.

_____

2 Write a check mark (✓) next to each sentence that is in the past tense.

6 points each

(1) Luis asked Mary to help him.   ____

(2) I clap for Tom.   ____

(3) Dad dressed for work.   ____

(4) The play ended late.   ____

(5) We fry eggs.   ____

3 Complete each sentence with a verb from the brackets.   5 points each

(1) I _____ every day.

[jog / jogs]

(2) You _____ eggs last week.

[cook / cooked]

(3) He _____ at any joke.

[grin / grins]

(4) She _____ her drink earlier.

[spill / spilled]

4 Complete each sentence with a verb from the box. Change the tense if necessary.   6 points each

| end   work   play   walk   help |

(1) Last week, we _____ to the park.

(2) When will this play _____?

(3) Ron _____ all the time.

(4) Yesterday, Dad _____ at his office.

(5) He _____ at home every day.

Super!

Adjectives

Date   /   /

Name

Level
★ ★ ★

Score
/100

1 Trace the adjective to complete each sentence.

5 points each

(1) The fruit is <u>round</u>.

(2) The donkeys are <u>brown</u>.

(3) The horn is <u>loud</u>.

(4) The pancake is <u>flat</u>.

Don't forget!

Words used to describe people, places, or things are called
adjectives. Adjectives are "describing" words.

---

2 Trace the adjectives to complete each sentence pair.

10 points each

(1) The shirt is <u>new</u>.
The shirt is <u>old</u>.

(2) The rope is <u>long</u>.
The rope is <u>short</u>.

(3) The boy runs <u>fast</u>.
The boy runs <u>slow</u>.

3   Match each sentence with its picture.   5 points each

(1) The train is long. •

(2) The train is short. •

(3) My dress is old. •

(4) My dress is wet. •

(5) My dress is blue. •

ⓐ

ⓑ

ⓒ

ⓓ

ⓔ

4   Complete each sentence with an adjective from the box.   5 points each

slow	old	round	loud	wet

(1) The dish is _____.

(2) The snail is _____.

(3) The rock music is _____.

(4) My rain boots are _____.

(5) Her grandmother is _____.

You are smart!

26 Adjectives

Level
★ ★ ★

Date / /

Name

Score
/100

1 Circle the adjective in each sentence.

6 points each

(1) The snake is long.

(2) The old shoes smell.

(3) I climbed a tall tree.

(4) The strawberries are sweet.

(5) My dress is wet.

2 Complete each sentence with an adjective from the brackets.

5 points each

(1) The button is _____ .
[small / long / high / brown]

(2) The frog is _____ .
[salty / tired / cold / green]

(3) The boy runs _____ .
[hot / fast / new / sweet]

(4) The table is _____ .
[sweet / round / square / fast]

3 Trace the adjectives to complete each sentence. Then circle the picture that matches each sentence.

5 points each

(1) The _tasty_ drink is _hot_.

ⓐ   ⓑ

(2) The _big_ tire is _flat_.

ⓐ   ⓑ

(3) The _young_ boy is _tired_.

ⓐ   ⓑ

(4) The _round_ cake is _purple_.

ⓐ   ⓑ

(5) The _tiny_ light is _bright_.

ⓐ   ⓑ

4 Complete each sentence with an adjective from the box.

5 points each

| fast | cold | high | tasty | frozen |

(1) I skate on a _frozen_ lake.

(2) I like to skate _____.

(3) The _____ air feels good.

(4) My teacher can jump _____.

(5) My Dad drinks some _____ hot cocoa.

You are clever.

53

Simple Sentences
Subject

27

Level

Date / /

Name

Score /100

1 Match the sentence parts.

5 points each

(1) The tigers •   •ⓐ flies away.

(2) The duck •   •ⓑ are sleeping.

(3) The frog •   •ⓒ jumps into the pond.

(4) The bird •   •ⓓ is swimming.

Don't forget!

The person or thing that is doing or being something in the sentence is the **subject** of the sentence.

For example: <u>The lion</u> roars.
        subject

---

2 Trace the subject to complete each sentence.

10 points each

(1) <u>Mom</u> is happy.

(2) <u>My sister</u> is driving.

(3) <u>The ball</u> bounced.

3 Circle the subject of each sentence.

6 points each

(1) (Two girls) have green skirts.

(2) My sock has a hole.

(3) The cats lick their paws.

(4) Most birds like worms.

(5) One boy brushes his hair.

4 Complete each sentence with a subject from the brackets.

5 points each

(1) _____ cooks dinner.

[Dad / The boys]

(2) _____ falls down.

[The girl / The beds]

(3) _____ jumps.

[A frog / The boys]

(4) _____ eat all the food.

[The television / I]

Very well done!

Date / /

Name

1 Match the sentence parts.

(1) **The hot soup**
(subject) •

• ⓐ flies away.

(2) **The messy room** •
(subject)

• ⓑ hops away.

(3) **The fast rabbit** •
(subject)

• ⓒ smells bad.

(4) **The old owl** •
(subject)

• ⓓ is red.

Don't forget!

Words that describe the subject of the sentence are sometimes included in the subject of the sentence.
For example: <u>The angry lions</u> roar.
subject

---

2 Trace the subject to complete each sentence. Then read the sentence aloud.

(1) <u>Two happy girls</u> play in the park.

(2) <u>Three old cars</u> sit in the lot.

(3) <u>My stinky socks</u> need washing.

3 Circle the subject of each sentence.

5 points each

(1) The cold water fills the tub.

(2) The sour lemons make good lemonade.

(3) The happy dog runs up the hill.

(4) The tall man got the bowl.

4 Complete each sentence with a subject from the box.

6 points each

Our silly dog	My lucky hat	The big book
The brown horse		The pretty flowers

(1) _____ keeps me warm.

(2) _____ smells everything.

(3) _____ bloomed today.

(4) _____ jumps up.

(5) _____ fell.

Great!

57

Simple Sentences
Predicate

29

Level ★★★

Date / /

Name

Score

/100

1 Trace the verb to complete each sentence.

3 points each

(1) My family <u>cooks</u>. (2) Nora <u>swims</u>.

(3) The tent <u>falls</u>. (4) Henry <u>runs</u>.

(5) Mom <u>sleeps</u>. (6) The girls <u>skip</u>.

(7) My teacher <u>draws</u>. (8) The sailboat <u>floats</u>.

(9) My sister <u>cheers</u>. (10) Jenny <u>talks</u>.

> **Don't forget!**
> The action part of the sentence is called the **predicate**. The verb is always in the predicate.
>   For example: The lions <u>roar</u>.
>   predicate

2 Find the predicate in each sentence and write it in the space provided.

5 points each

(1) The children read. _____

(2) The school bells ring. _____

(3) His pencil breaks. _____

(4) The button pops. _____

58   © Kumon Publishing Co., Ltd.

3 Match the sentence parts.

6 points each

SUBJECTS

(1) Her dress •

(2) The cowboy •

(3) Jose's hat •

(4) The girl •

(5) The cats •

PREDICATES

ⓐ • rides.

ⓑ • fits.

ⓒ • eat.

ⓓ • falls.

ⓔ • sings.

4 Complete each sentence with a predicate from the box.

5 points each

| float | plays | rings | waves |

(1) The phone _____.

(2) The boats _____.

(3) Our band _____.

(4) My mom _____.

Good thinking!

Simple Sentences
Predicate

Level

Date / /

Name

Score /100

---

1 Trace the predicate to complete each sentence.

5 points each

(1) She <u>eats chips</u>.

(2) Nora <u>runs the track</u>.

(3) Dad <u>takes a nap</u>.

> **Don't forget!**
> Words that describe the action are also included in the **predicate**.
> For example: He <u>opens the door</u>.
> predicate

2 Find the predicate in each sentence and write it in the space provided.

5 points each

(1) Tom ate pizza. _____

(2) Valerie reads a book. _____

(3) The bird flew away. _____

(4) We play tag. _____

(5) The girl jumped and danced.

_____

3 Complete each sentence with a predicate from the brackets. 5 points each

(1) The rabbit _____.
[jumps far / runs up a tree]

(2) The iron _____.
[goes to sleep / is very hot]

(3) Julie _____.
[sang loudly / flew up]

(4) The scout _____.
[breaks sticks / helped the lady]

4 Complete each sentence with a predicate from the box. 10 points each

ran fast	is clean
sings a song	get up early

(1) My room _____.

(2) Grandma _____.

(3) I _____.

(4) Bill _____.

Very good!

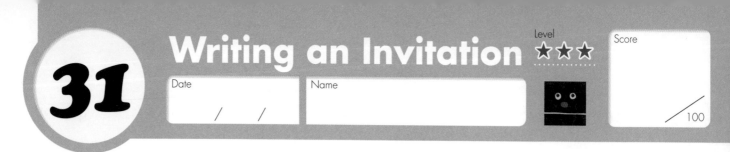

31 Writing an Invitation ★★★

Level

Score

Date / /

Name

/100

1 Trace the words to complete the invitation.

6 points each

(1) Dear Tom ,
[WHO]

(2) Please come to my party .
[WHAT]

(3) We will go to the pool .
[WHERE]

(4) It is on Friday and starts
[WHEN:DAY]

at three o'clock .
[WHEN:TIME]

(5) Sincerely ,
[CLOSING]

Tim
[NAME]

2 Complete the invitation with the information from the box.

4 points each

(1) Dear _____ ,
[WHO]

(2) Please come to my _____ .
[WHAT]

(3) It is on _____ at
[WHEN: DAY]

_____ .
[WHEN: TIME]

(4) Meet us _____ .
[WHERE]

(5) _____ ,
[CLOSING]

Jim

WHO:
Clark
WHAT:
party
DAY:
Saturday
TIME:
one o'clock
WHERE:
in the park
CLOSING:
From

3 Complete the invitation with the words from the box.

5 points each

Dear party come park play cake Sincerely

(1) _____ Joanna,

(2) Please _____ to my _____ on Saturday at two o'clock.

(3) We will _____ tag and eat _____ in the _____.

(4) _____,

Nicole

4 Complete the invitation in your own words. Sign your name at the bottom.

30 points for completion

Dear _____,
[WHO]
Please come to my _____
[WHAT]
on _____ at _____ o'clock.
[WHEN: DAY]　　[WHEN: TIME]
We will go to _____.
[WHERE]
Thank you!

_____,
[CLOSING]

_____
[YOUR NAME]

Lovely invitation!

32

Writing a Thank-You Letter ★★★

Level

Date / /

Name

Score
/100

1 Trace the words to complete the thank-you letter below.

5 points each

(1) <u>Dear Max</u>,
   [WHO]

(2) <u>Thank you for</u> the ball.
   [WHAT]

(3) <u>I like</u> to play with it.
   [WHY]
   It is fun.

(4) <u>Your friend</u>,
   [CLOSING]
   Jen
   [NAME]

2 Complete the thank-you letter with the words from the box.

5 points each

| like   bike   Dear   From   you |

(1) _____ Grandpa,
   [WHO]

(2) Thank ____ for the ____.
   [WHAT]

(3) I ____ to ride it.
   [WHY]
   I can bike quickly now.

(4) _____,
   [CLOSING]
   Gus
   [NAME]

64   © Kumon Publishing Co., Ltd.

3 Complete the thank-you letter with the words from the box.

10 points each

| train   Sincerely   Dear   Thank |

(1) _____ Tim,

(2) _____ you for the _____.

I really like to push it through the tunnel.

(3) _____ ,

Gary

4 Complete the thank-you letter in your own words. Sign your name at the bottom.

30 points for completion

Dear _____ ,
　　　　　　[WHO]
Thank you for _____ .
　　　　　　　　　　[WHAT]
I like _____ .
　　　　　　　　　　[WHY]

_____ ,
　　[CLOSING]

_____
　　[YOUR NAME]

What a nice letter!

65

Writing a Story

1 Complete each sentence with a word or words from the box. Then read the passage aloud.

5 points each

pig home hay easy made

Three pigs wanted safe homes.

(1) The first _pig_ made a home with _hay_.

(2) The second pig _____ a _____ with sticks.

(3) The homes were _____ to make.

2 Complete each sentence with a subject or predicate from the boxes. Then read the passage aloud.

5 points each

The third pig   It

went to the first home
was hard work

(1) _____ made a brick home.

_____ was not easy to make.

(2) The brick home _____.

Then a wolf came. The wolf wanted to catch the pigs.

(3) The wolf _____.

3 Complete each sentence with a word or words from the box. Then read the passage aloud.

7 points each

wolf	puff	hair	first	pig
home	help	stick	run	huffed

The _____(1) pig was in his hay home.

The _____(2) said, "I will catch you, _____(3)."

The pig said, "Not by the _____(4)

on my chinny-chin-chin."

The wolf said, "Then I will huff.

I will _____(5)."

So the wolf _____(6). He puffed.

Soon, the hay _____(7) fell.

"Help, _____(8)!" the first pig said.

"I must _____(9) away!"

The first pig ran to the

_____(10) home.

Not by the hair on my chinny-chin-chin.

I will catch you, pig.

Help, help!

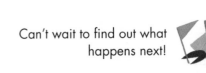

Can't wait to find out what happens next!

67

34

Writing a Story

Level ★★★

Score

/100

Date / /

Name

1 Complete each sentence with a subject or predicate from the boxes. Then read the passage aloud. 5 points each

| The second pig   He   I | will puff   puffed |

The wolf went to the stick home.

(1) _____ said, "I can catch you, pig."

(2) _____ said, "Not by the hair on my chinny-chin-chin."

(3) The wolf said, "__ will huff. I _____ ."

(4) So the wolf huffed. He _____ .

2 Complete each sentence with a word or words from the box. 5 points each

| stick   pigs   brick   home   run |

(1) Soon, the _____ home fell, too.

(2) "We must _____ away!" the pigs said.

(3) The _____ ran to the brick home.

(4) The wolf went to the _____ _____ , too.

3 Complete the story with the missing words. Then read the passage aloud.

5 points each

The wolf _____(1)_____, "I can _____(2)_____ _____(3)_____, pigs."

The third _____(4)_____ said,

"Not by the _____(5)_____

on my chinny-chin-_____(6)_____."

Not by the hair on my chinny-chin-chin.

I can catch you, pigs.

_____(7)_____ _____(8)_____ said, "Then I

will huff. I will puff."

So the wolf _____(9)_____. He puffed.

This is hard work!

But the _____(10)_____ home was OK.

"This is hard _____(11)_____!"

the wolf said.

The tired wolf left.

We are safe!

"We are _____(12)_____!" said the pigs.

Did you read it aloud? What a good story!

35

Review

Date / /

Name

Level

Score

/100

1 Complete each sentence with a word from the box.

6 points each

| The   An   All   Yes   This |

(1) _____ best dogs don't bark.

(2) _____ ant is small but strong.

(3) _____ is the best ice cream.

(4) "_____," Jerome agreed.

(5) _____ of the kids danced.

2 Replace the noun in each sentence with a pronoun from the box.

5 points each

| She   It   He   They |

(1) The boy runs.   _____ runs.

(2) The girl wins.   _____ wins.

(3) The ants eat the cake. _____ eat the cake.

(4) That tree is tall.   _____ is tall.

3 Replace the noun in each sentence with a pronoun from the box. Capitalize letters when necessary.

5 points each

mine	hers	your	his

(1) Tim has a dog. The dog is _____ dog.

(2) You have a red shirt. _____ shirt is red.

(3) She has a cat. The cat is_____.

(4) I have candy. The candy is_____.

4 Rewrite the letters below as a sentence with correct spacing, punctuation, and capital letters.

5 points each

(1) isthatyourhouse _____

(2) iamtired _____

(3) whereisthedog _____

(4) thelionroared _____

(5) thatisreallyexciting _____

(6) thatbeestungme _____

You are almost done!

36

Review

Date / /

Name

Level ★★★

Score

/100

1 Complete each sentence with a verb from the brackets.   *6 points each*

(1) The boys _____ in the park.   [run / runs]

(2) Lana _____ a big meal.   [cook / cooks]

(3) The play _____ on time.   [end / ends]

(4) You _____ a good buddy.   [am / are / is]

(5) I _____ not tall.   [am / are / is]

2 Complete each sentence with a verb from the brackets.   *5 points each*

(1) Now we _____ up and down.
[jump / jumps / jumped]

(2) Mom _____ at us yesterday morning.
[wave / waves / waved]

(3) I _____ dad for help yesterday.
[ask / asks / asked]

(4) James _____ his teeth every day.
[brush / brushes]

3 Write each sentence with a subject and predicate from each box.
End each sentence with a period.

5 points each

| My ice cream   We |
| The little dog   My mom |

| are dancing   licked me |
| spilled the water   melts |

(1) _____

(2) _____

(3) _____

(4) _____

4 Complete the invitation in your own words. Sign your name at
the bottom.

30 points for completion

Dear _____ ,
       [WHO]
Please come to my _____
                   [WHAT]
on _____ at _____ o'clock.
    [WHEN: DAY]   [WHEN: TIME]
We will go to _____ .
                   [WHERE]
Thank you!

_____ ,
[CLOSING]

_____
[YOUR NAME]

Congratulations!
You finished!

(1) Vocabulary: Short Vowel Sounds pp 2,3

(1)
(1) bag (2) bug (3) cat (4) cut (5) hot
(6) hit (7) tin (8) ten (9) pot (10) pit
(11) fun (12) fin

(2) (1) ⓒ (2) ⓐ (3) ⓓ (4) ⓑ

(3)
(1) bat (2) fun (3) ten
(4) pot (5) dig (6) fin

(4) (1) bug (2) pen (3) hat (4) pig

(2) Vocabulary: Consonant Combinations pp 4,5

(1)
(1) ⓗ (2) ⓑ (3) ⓓ (4) ⓐ
(5) ⓕ (6) ⓒ (7) ⓖ (8) ⓔ

(2)
(1) frog (2) flag (3) crab
(4) clock (5) brick (6) plant

(3)
(1) ⓓ (2) ⓔ (3) ⓐ
(4) ⓕ (5) ⓑ (6) ⓒ

(4)
(1) snow (2) sky (3) skip
(4) smell (5) ski

(3) Vocabulary: Consonant Combinations pp 6,7

(1)
(1) ⓒ (2) ⓑ (3) ⓐ (4) ⓕ
(5) ⓖ (6) ⓔ (7) ⓓ

(2)
(1) wheel (2) chin (3) thin
(4) shark (5) three (6) chop
(7) ship

(3)
(1) hand (2) sick (3) lunch
(4) whale (5) thick (6) fish
(7) band (8) chair

(4)
(1) lunch (2) sand (3) chair
(4) band (5) whale

(4) Vocabulary: Long Vowel Sounds pp 8,9

(1)
(1) ⓑ (2) ⓓ (3) ⓐ (4) ⓕ
(5) ⓔ (6) ⓒ

(2)
(1) plane (2) bay (3) brain
(4) day (5) cane (6) rain

(3)
(1) ⓐ (2) ⓓ (3) ⓒ (4) ⓑ
(5) ⓔ

(4)
(1) bee (2) heat (3) three
(4) sea (5) feet

(5) Vocabulary: Long Vowel Sounds pp 10,11

(1)
(1) hide (2) cry (3) kite
(4) slide (5) hike (6) five

(2)
(1) five (2) cry (3) hike
(4) hide (5) slide (6) kite

(3)
(1) ⓔ (2) ⓖ (3) ⓒ (4) ⓓ
(5) ⓑ (6) ⓕ (7) ⓐ

(4)
(1) goat (2) boat (3) rose
(4) bone (5) rope (6) road

(6) Vocabulary: Long Vowel Sounds pp 12,13

(1)
(1) ⓓ (2) ⓒ (3) ⓖ (4) ⓐ
(5) ⓕ (6) ⓔ (7) ⓑ

(2)
(1) glue (2) dune (3) cube

(3)
(1) glue (2) bay (3) boat (4) three
(5) bike (6) brain (7) five (8) road

(4)
(1) nose (2) sky (3) train (4) wheel

7 Sight Words

pp 14, 15

1 (1) The (2) The (3) This (4) This

2

3 (1) A (2) A (3) An (4) An (5) All (6) All

4

all	an	a
all	all	an
an	a	all

5
(1) a b x l y all x b   all
(2) p x t r h m this   this
(3) b y o o k l an p b   an
(4) u i w the l m n r   the

8 Sight Words

pp 16, 17

1 (1) a / Yes (2) a / No
(3) all / not (4) a / Yes

2 (1) No (2) Yes (3) Yes (4) No

3
(1) I sat on the chair.
(2) Do you want an apple?
(3) Is this my hat?
(4) No, not all birds can fly.
(5) Yes, she likes to read.
(6) There is no soap.

4 (1) this (2) an (3) all (4) a

9 Punctuation

pp 18, 19

1 (1) The / . (2) The / . (3) Cats / .
(4) Saturday / . (5) The / . (6) Amy / .

2
(1) All dogs bark.
(2) I like to eat fish.
(3) Soccer is fun.
(4) The sun is yellow.
(5) The tent was wet.

3 My shirt is black.   That's my favorite
the bat scared me   I like candy.
you have a dog   Bob is funny.
My doll is broken   lemons are not. sweet

4 The sun is out today. It is hot.
We want to play tag with Timmy.
That would be fun.
The game is starting.
Timmy fell down.
I hope he is okay.
He is fine.
We can play again.

10 Punctuation

pp 20, 21

1
(1) The dog barks.
(2) Is this your pen?
(3) Is that my hat?
(4) That bee stung me!
(5) I hit my leg!

2 (1) ? / . (2) ! / ? (3) ? / . (4) ? / .

3 (1) . (2) ! (3) ? (4) ! (5) .

4
(1) That dog bit me!
(2) The toy broke! (or The toy broke.)
(3) Do not touch the fire!
(4) Is it time for bed?
(5) I like carrots.

75

11 Nouns: Singular

1 (1) pig   (2) cow   (3) pen   (4) bike
(5) girl   (6) boy   (7) truck   (8) train
(9) lion   (10) bee

2 (1) ⓒ / The <u>cow</u> moos.
(2) ⓐ / The <u>tiger</u> hunts.
(3) ⓑ / The <u>girl</u> plays.

3 (1) panda   (2) boy   (3) car
(4) lion   (5) truck   (6) train

4 (1) The <u>lion</u> sleeps.   (2) The <u>boy</u> walks.
(3) The <u>girl</u> plays.   (4) The <u>cat</u> climbs.
(5) The <u>bike</u> is red.

12 Nouns: Plural
pp 24,25

1 (1) dogs   (2) girls   (3) pigs
(4) pens   (5) cars   (6) balls
(7) ants   (8) cows

2 crabs, rabbits, lamps, spoons, coins

3 (1) pigs   (2) cow   (3) pandas
(4) bike   (5) girl   (6) boys
(7) swans   (8) car   (9) lions
(10) frog   (11) teacher   (12) pen

4 (1) pandas   (2) cow   (3) girls
(4) books   (5) cars

13 Pronouns
pp 26,27

1 (1) I   (2) He   (3) She
(4) They   (5) It

2 (1) ⓐ   (2) ⓓ   (3) ⓑ   (4) ⓒ

3 (1) She   (2) They   (3) He
(4) It

4 (1) It   (2) She   (3) He   (4) They

14 Pronouns
pp 28,29

1 (1) I / my   (2) She / her
(3) He / his   (4) You / your

2 (1) his   (2) my
(3) her   (4) your

3 (1) I / mine   (2) She / hers
(3) He / his   (4) You / yours

4 (1) yours   (2) hers   (3) his
(4) mine

15 Pronouns
pp 30,31

1 (1) ⓒ   (2) ⓐ   (3) ⓑ   (4) ⓓ

2 (1) me   (2) you
(3) her   (4) him

3 (1) We   (2) They
(3) We   (4) They

4 (1) they   (2) her   (3) We
(4) you   (5) him   (6) me

16 Verbs: Singular
pp 32,33

1 (1) drinks   (2) eats   (3) runs
(4) jumps   (5) blows   (6) rows

2 (1) grows   (2) chops
(3) pops   (4) rides

3 (1) ⓐ   (2) ⓔ   (3) ⓑ   (4) ⓓ   (5) ⓒ

4 (1) sleeps   (2) runs   (3) roars
(4) digs   (5) jumps

17 Verbs: Plural
pp 34,35

1 (1) smile (2) smell (3) jump (4) break
(5) roar (6) sing (7) ride

2 The drink spills. (The hot dogs fall.)
(The frogs jump.) The trumpet blows.
(The stars shine.) (The ballerinas turn.)

3 (1) ⓒ (2) ⓐ (3) ⓓ (4) ⓑ

4 (1) sleeps (2) play (3) feel
(4) reads (5) land (6) drives

18 Verbs: Singular and Plural
pp 36,37

1 (1) ⓑ (2) ⓓ (3) ⓐ (4) ⓒ

2 (1) shine (2) sleeps (3) eats
(4) land (5) hunts

3 (1) falls (2) runs
(3) play (4) floats

4 (1) bees (2) cone (3) spots
(4) hogs (5) bag (6) ants

19 Verbs: First and Third Person
pp 38,39

1 (1) run (2) jump (3) sleep
(4) hit (5) fall

2 (1) cook (2) fall (3) eat
(4) find (5) read

3 (1) falls (2) runs (3) jumps
(4) stops (5) hurts

4 (1) yells (2) sleeps (3) cooks
(4) eats (5) breaks (6) moves

20 Verbs: First, Second, and Third Person
pp 40,41

1 (1) run (2) stop (3) sleep
(4) like (5) ride

2 (1) cook (2) use (3) drink
(4) hide (5) eat (6) read

3 (1) sleep (2) run (3) sit
(4) trip (5) jumps (6) drinks

4 (1) play (2) looks (3) drops
(4) like (5) swims

21 Verbs: Am / Are / Is
pp 42,43

1 (1) am (2) are (3) is (4) is

2 (1) am (2) am (3) are (4) are
(5) is (6) is

3 (1) ⓒ (2) ⓐ (3) ⓓ (4) ⓑ

4 (1) am (2) is (3) are
(4) am (5) is

22 Verbs: Present and Past Tense
pp 44,45

1 (1) stops (2) sleeps
(3) wins (4) shaves

2 (1) waved (2) cooked (3) wanted
(4) jumped (5) played

3 (1) want<u>ed</u> (2) paint<u>ed</u> (3) talk<u>ed</u>
(4) walk<u>ed</u> (5) add<u>ed</u> (6) wait<u>ed</u>

4 (1) want (2) shared
(3) played (4) walked

77

23 Verbs: Present and Past Tense
pp 46,47

1 (1) collected (2) sailed
(3) worked

2 (1) walked (2) cooked
(3) jumped (4) brushed

3 (1) ⓓ (2) ⓒ (3) ⓐ (4) ⓑ

4 (1) helped (2) call
(3) pulled (4) tripped
(5) poke

24 Review: Verbs
pp 48,49

1 (1) The girls painted.
(2) Mom dusted the chair.
(3) The show ended.
(4) Billy added one and one.

2 (1) ✓ (3) ✓ (4) ✓

3 (1) jog (2) cooked
(3) grins (4) spilled

4 (1) walked (2) end
(3) plays (4) worked
(5) helps

25 Adjectives
pp 50,51

1 (1) round (2) brown
(3) loud (4) flat

2 (1) new / old (2) long / short
(3) fast / slow

3 (1) ⓔ (2) ⓐ (3) ⓒ (4) ⓑ (5) ⓓ

4 (1) round (2) slow
(3) loud (4) wet
(5) old

26 Adjectives
pp 52,53

1 (1) The snake is ⟨long⟩.
(2) The ⟨old⟩ shoes smell.
(3) I climbed a ⟨tall⟩ tree.
(4) The strawberries are ⟨sweet⟩.
(5) My dress is ⟨wet⟩.

2 (1) small (2) green
(3) fast (4) round

3 (1) ⓑ (2) ⓐ (3) ⓐ (4) ⓑ (5) ⓐ

4 (1) frozen (2) fast
(3) cold (4) high
(5) tasty

27 Simple Sentences: Subject
pp 54,55

1 (1) ⓑ (2) ⓓ (3) ⓒ (4) ⓐ

2 (1) Mom (2) My sister
(3) The ball

3 (1) ⟨Two girls⟩ have green skirts.
(2) ⟨My sock⟩ has a hole.
(3) ⟨The cats⟩ lick their paws.
(4) ⟨Most birds⟩ like worms.
(5) ⟨One boy⟩ brushes his hair.

4 (1) Dad (2) The girl
(3) A frog (4) I

28 Simple Sentences: Subject
pp 56,57

1 (1) ⓓ (2) ⓒ (3) ⓑ (4) ⓐ

2 (1) Two happy girls
(2) Three old cars
(3) My stinky socks

3 (1) ⟨The cold water⟩ fills the tub.
(2) ⟨The sour lemons⟩ make good lemonade.
(3) ⟨The happy dog⟩ runs up the hill.
(4) ⟨The tall man⟩ got the bowl.

4
(1) My lucky hat
(2) Our silly dog
(3) The pretty flowers
(4) The brown horse
(5) The big book

29 Simple Sentences: Predicate
pp 58,59

1
(1) cooks
(2) swims
(3) falls
(4) runs
(5) sleeps
(6) skip
(7) draws
(8) floats
(9) cheers
(10) talks

2
(1) read
(2) ring
(3) breaks
(4) pops

3
(1) ⓑ
(2) ⓐ
(3) ⓓ
(4) ⓔ
(5) ⓒ

4
(1) rings
(2) float
(3) plays
(4) waves

30 Simple Sentences: Predicate
pp 60,61

1
(1) eats chips
(2) runs the track
(3) takes a nap

2
(1) ate pizza
(2) reads a book
(3) flew away
(4) play tag
(5) jumped and danced

3
(1) jumps far
(2) is very hot
(3) sang loudly
(4) helped the lady

4
(1) is clean
(2) sings a song
(3) get up early
(4) ran fast

31 Writing an Invitation
pp 62,63

1
(1) Dear Tom
(2) come to my party
(3) go to the pool
(4) Friday / at three o'clock
(5) Sincerely

2
(1) Clark
(2) party
(3) Saturday / one o'clock
(4) in the park
(5) From

3
(1) Dear
(2) come / party
(3) play / cake / park
(4) Sincerely

4 [ANSWERS MAY VARY]

32 Writing a Thank-You Letter
pp 64,65

1
(1) Dear Max
(2) Thank you for
(3) I like
(4) Your friend

2
(1) Dear
(2) you / bike
(3) like
(4) From

3
(1) Dear
(2) Thank / train
(3) Sincerely

4 [ANSWERS MAY VARY]

33 Writing a Story
pp 66,67

1
(1) pig / hay
(2) made / home
(3) easy

2
(1) The third pig / It
(2) was hard work
(3) went to the first home

3
(1) first (2) wolf
(3) pig (4) hair
(5) puff (6) huffed
(7) home (8) help
(9) run (10) stick

34 Writing a Story
pp 68,69

1
(1) He
(2) The second pig
(3) I / will puff
(4) puffed

2
(1) stick (2) run
(3) pigs (4) brick / home

3
(1) said (2) catch
(3) you (4) pig
(5) hair (6) chin
(7) The (8) wolf
(9) huffed (10) brick
(11) work (12) safe

35 Review
pp 70,71

1
(1) The (2) An
(3) This (4) Yes
(5) All

2
(1) He (2) She
(3) They (4) It

3
(1) his (2) Your
(3) hers (4) mine

4
(1) Is that your house?
(2) I am tired.
(3) Where is the dog?
(4) The lion roared.
(5) That is really exciting!
(6) That bee stung me!

36 Review
pp 72,73

1
(1) run (2) cooks
(3) ends (4) are
(5) am

2
(1) jump (2) waved
(3) asked (4) brushes

3
(1) My ice cream melts.
(2) The little dog licked me.
(3) My mom spilled the water.
(4) We are dancing.

4 [ANSWERS MAY VARY]